HOLIDAYS, FESTIVALS, & CELEBRATIONS

SAINT PATRICK'S DAY

BY ANN HEINRICHS · ILLUSTRATED BY JOEL SNYDER

Published in the United States of America by The Child's World®
PO Box 326 • Chanhassen, MN 55317-0326
800-599-READ • www.childsworld.com

ACKNOWLEDGMENTS
The Child's World®: Mary Berendes, Publishing Director

Editorial Directions, Inc.: E. Russell Primm, Editorial Director; Katie Marsico, Managing Editor; Judith Shiffer,
Assistant Editor; Caroline Wood and Rory Mabin, Editorial Assistants; Susan Hindman, Copy Editor and
Proofreader; Elizabeth Nellums, Rory Mabin, Ruth Martin, and Caroline Wood, Fact Checkers; Tim Griffin/
IndexServ, Indexer

The Design Lab: Kathleen Petelinsek, Design and Page Production

LIBRARY OF CONGRESS CATALOGING-IN-PUBLICATION DATA
Heinrichs, Ann.
  Saint Patrick's Day / by Ann Heinrichs ; illustrated by Joel Snyder.
    p. cm. — (Holidays, festivals, & celebrations)
  Includes index.
  ISBN 1-59296-581-4 (library bound : alk. paper)
  1. Saint Patrick's Day—Juvenile literature. I. Snyder, Joel, ill.
  II. Title. III. Series.
  GT4995.P3H45 2006
  394.262—dc22   2005025687

TABLE OF CONTENTS

CHAPTER ONE

HAPPY SAINT PATRICK'S DAY!

Bands are marching down the street. The sound of bagpipes fills the air. And everyone is wearing green. It's Saint Patrick's Day!

Saint Patrick's Day is a joyful holiday. It's a time to celebrate being Irish. But you don't have to be Irish to join in. People like to say "Everyone's Irish on Saint Patrick's Day!"

Would you like to learn a Saint Patrick's Day greeting? Just say, "*Erin go bragh* (EHR-in go BRAH)!" It means "Ireland forever!"

Listen to the bagpipes! It must be Saint Patrick's Day.

WHO WAS SAINT PATRICK?

S aint Patrick is the **patron saint** of Ireland. He lived more than 1,500 years ago. Patrick was born in Great Britain. When he was sixteen, outlaws kidnapped him. They sold him as a slave in Ireland. There he tended sheep for his master.

Patrick was kidnapped and sold into slavery in Ireland.
Once there, he worked as a shepherd.

While a slave, Patrick's faith grew stronger. One day, he escaped. Then he became a Christian missionary. Patrick traveled through much of Ireland. He spread his faith wherever he went.

Many Irish people believed in several gods then. But Patrick taught about the one God. He was often in danger for his teachings. But he bravely kept on. The Irish people loved him for his kindness. And they still love him today!

Saint Patrick's Day is March 17. That's believed to be the date of Patrick's death.

Patrick preached Christianity throughout Ireland.

CHAPTER THREE

THE LEGEND OF
THE SNAKES

Many legends, or tales, were created about Saint Patrick. One legend says that snakes covered the land. Saint Patrick stood high on a hill. With his wooden staff, he drove the snakes into the sea. At last, Ireland was safe.

This story probably has a hidden meaning. The snakes stand for Ireland's old religions. Saint Patrick drove them out with Christianity.

Ireland is an island. Beautiful green grass covers the hillsides. That's why Ireland is called the Emerald Isle.

According to popular legend, Saint Patrick drove the snakes out of Ireland.

AN IRISH BLESSING

May there always be work
for your hands to do,
May your purse always
hold a coin or two.
May the sun always
shine warm on your
windowpane,
May a rainbow be certain
to follow each rain.
May the hand of a friend
always be near you,
And may God fill your
heart with gladness to
cheer you.
—Author unknown

CHAPTER FOUR

SAINT PATRICK AND THE SHAMROCK

Another legend tells about the shamrock. That's a three-leaf clover. Saint Patrick used it to explain the Trinity—the Father, Son, and Holy Spirit. All three, he said, are God. Yet there is only one God.

In the same way, shamrocks have three leaves. But they grow on just one stem. People welcomed this lesson. Now people wear shamrocks on Saint Patrick's Day. The shamrock is still an important **symbol** of Ireland.

The shamrock is the national plant of Ireland.

Saint Patrick used the shamrock as a symbol for the Trinity.

SAINT PATRICK'S GREEN

Oh, I love to see the
   shamrocks
Boys wear March seventeen,
And I love the girls' green
   ribbons,
And bits of evergreen;
For they stand for brave
   Saint Patrick,
So fearless and so good—
Oh! The Irish ought
   to love him,
Just as everybody should!
—Bertha E. Bush
   (early 1900s–?)

CHAPTER FIVE

A GRAND HOLIDAY

Many Irish people came to the American colonies. They brought their customs to their new home. One was celebrating Saint Patrick's Day!

This holiday began as a religious feast. But it quickly became a big public event. Boston, Massachusetts, celebrated Saint Patrick's Day in 1737. New York City held a parade in 1762. Soon other cities joined in.

The parades were grand affairs. Irish clubs provided marching bands. Firefighters and police officers joined in, too. So did the mayor and other leaders. It was a great day for the Irish!

Saint Patrick's Day parades have long been a holiday tradition in U.S. cities.

THE LUCK OF THE IRISH

May the luck of the Irish
And lots of good cheer
Bring a lift to your heart
That will last through the year.
—Author unknown

CHAPTER SIX

SYMBOLS AND DECORATIONS

Shamrocks are everywhere on Saint Patrick's Day. You'll see four-leaf clovers, too. They're signs of good luck. People often speak of the "luck of the Irish."

Leprechauns (LEP-ruh-kahnz) are favorite decorations. These magical little men hide in the forest. What if you catch a leprechaun? He must lead you to his pot of gold! It's hidden at the end of a rainbow.

Shillelaghs (shuh-LAY-leez) are Irish symbols, too. These sturdy sticks were once used for protection.

The harp is another Irish symbol. It's sometimes called the Brian Boru harp. Brian Boru was an Irish king. He lived about one thousand years ago. He brought the Irish nation together.

Leprechauns are a famous symbol for Saint Patrick's Day.

*A leprechaun is
   small and green—
He hides where he
   cannot be seen.
But if you catch one
   on this day,
He must give his gold away!
—Author unknown*

CHAPTER SEVEN

HOW WE CELEBRATE

Y ou'd better wear green on Saint Patrick's Day. If you don't, people can pinch you! You'll see green everywhere that day. It stands for Ireland, the Emerald Isle.

Ouch! Wear green on Saint Patrick's Day to avoid getting pinched.

Saint Patrick's Day parades are noisy! Floats and marching bands go by. Some bands play bagpipes. The musicians are wearing **kilts.** Other bands play loud brass horns. And booming drums keep a marching beat.

The crowds are a sea of green. People are wearing green hats and clothes. They're shouting "Erin go bragh!" Everyone is Irish today!

Corned beef and cabbage are **traditional** holiday foods. So are Irish stew and soda bread. They make a hearty meal after the parade.

Soda bread and Irish stew are traditional Irish foods.

Leprechauns peeking
Around a willow tree,
Pussy willows waking,
Longing to be free.
Colleens and shamrocks
And castles old and gray,
Put them all together
To make Saint Patrick's Day!
—Author unknown

CHAPTER EIGHT

SAINT PATRICK'S DAY AROUND THE WORLD

I rish people live all over the world. They love to celebrate Saint Patrick's Day. Even some cities in Asia celebrate.

Ireland is a festive place that day. Many people wear a little bunch of shamrocks. Dublin, Ireland's capital, holds the Saint Patrick's Festival. It lasts a whole week! There are parades, music, and fireworks.

New York City's parade is the largest in the world. More than 150,000 people take part. Chicago, Illinois, has a big parade, too. The city dyes the Chicago River green!

Saint Patrick's Day is popular all over the world.

SAINT PATRICK'S DAY POEM

Saint Patrick came from Ireland,
A country trimmed with green.
It has the shamrocks
    and the pipes—
Those leprechauns you've seen.
Those leprechauns will trip you—
You'll fall flat on your face.
They'll tickle your nose and
    sour the milk,
Then find a hiding place!
—Author unknown

THE POETS' CORNER

I'll Wear a Shamrock

Saint Patrick's Day is with us,
The day when all that's seen
To right and left and everywhere
Is green, green, green!

And Irish tunes they whistle
And Irish songs they sing,
Today each Irish lad walks out
As proud as any king.

I'll wear a four-leaf shamrock
In my coat, the glad day through,
For my father and mother are Irish
And I am Irish, too!

—Mary Carolyn Davies
(1888–1966)

Leprechaun, Leprechaun

Leprechaun, leprechaun, fly across the sea
And fetch an emerald shamrock for you and me.
Do not bring a nettle or a thistle for a joke,
But bring an Irish shamrock, for we are Irish folk.
And you and I, my leprechaun, will wear the shamrock gay,
And match it with an Irish smile upon Saint Patrick's Day!

—Author unknown

Saint Patrick's Day

I'm Looking Over a Four-Leaf Clover

I'm looking over a four-leaf clover
That I overlooked before.
One leaf is sunshine, the second is rain,
Third is the roses that grow in the lane.
No need explaining, the one remaining
Is somebody I adore.
I'm looking over a four-leaf clover
That I overlooked before.

—Song; words by Mort Dixon
(1892–1956)

Joining in the Spirit of Saint Patrick's Day

- Look at a map of the world. Can you find Ireland? Is it larger or smaller than your state?

- Do you know someone with an Irish background? Ask about his or her family history.

- Write an Irish blessing. It should be full of good wishes. Begin each line with "May you . . ." or "May your . . ."

- Does your city have a Saint Patrick's Day parade? Go and enjoy the fun!

IRELAND

SCOTLAND

IRISH
SEA

ENGLAND

IRELAND

ATLANTIC
OCEAN

NORTH
SEA

EUROPE

MEDITERRANEAN
SEA

N
W E
S

Making Irish Soda Bread

Ingredients:
2 cups all-purpose flour
1 cup whole wheat flour
2 teaspoons baking powder
½ teaspoon salt
½ cup sugar
2 eggs
1 ½ cups buttermilk or plain yogurt
¾ cup raisins
Cooking spray or a stick of butter/margarine

Directions:
Preheat the oven to 350 degrees Fahrenheit.* Place the baking powder, salt, sugar, and both kinds of flour in a bowl. Stir in the eggs and buttermilk (or yogurt). Add the raisins and stir again. Next, sprinkle a little flour onto a baking board or some other clean, flat surface. Pour your doughy mixture onto this surface and knead ten times. Use your hands to shape the dough into a loaf. Finally, grease a loaf pan with cooking spray or a small amount of butter (or margarine). Place the loaf in the pan and cook for one hour. Allow the bread to cool before removing it from the pan. When it's ready, your taste treat should feed about twelve people—and maybe a few leprechauns!

Have an adult help you operate the oven.

Making a Pot o' Gold

*Those tricky leprechauns never let you get near their
pots of gold, so how about making your own?*

What you need:

A paper plate
A cardboard tube (empty toilet paper roll or paper towel roll)
Glue
Paint or markers
Gold glitter
Scissors

Instructions:

1. Cut down the toilet paper roll or paper towel roll so it is about 2 inches high.
2. Paint or color it black.
3. Cut the paper plate in half.
4. Next, cut out a rainbow shape from the outside edge of one half of the plate. Make sure the end of the rainbow shape will fit inside the painted cardboard tube.
5. Paint or color the rainbow-shaped cutout so that it has all the colors of a rainbow.
6. When the paint or marker ink is dry, put one end of your rainbow inside the black cardboard tube. Glue it in place.
7. Put some glue on the top edge of the cardboard tube and sprinkle gold glitter on top of the glue. Let the glue dry.

*Now you have your very own pot of gold at the end of a rainbow.
Happy Saint Patrick's Day!*

Words to Know

colleens (*kol-LEENZ*) Irish girls

colonies (*KOL-uh-neez*) lands with ties to another country

emerald (*EM-uh-ruld*) a green jewel

kilts (*KILTZ*) pleated skirts sometimes worn by Irish and Scottish men

patron saint (*PAY-truhn SAYNT*) a holy person special to a group of people

symbol (*SIM-buhl*) an object that stands for an idea

traditional (*truh-DISH-uhn-uhl*) following old customs

How to Learn More about Saint Patrick's Day

At the Library

Gnojewski, Carol. *St. Patrick's Day Crafts.* Berkeley Heights, N.J.:
   Enslow Publishers, 2004.

Krull, Kathleen, and David McPhail (illustrator). *A Pot o' Gold:
   A Treasury of Irish Stories, Poetry, Folklore, and (of Course) Blarney.*
   New York: Hyperion Books for Children, 2004.

Nolan, Janet, and Ben F. Stahl. *The St. Patrick's Day Shillelagh.*
   Morton Grove, Ill.: Albert Whitman & Company, 2002.

Wojciechowski, Susan, and Tom Curry (illustrator). *A Fine St.
   Patrick's Day.* New York: Random House, 2004.

On the Web

Visit our home page for lots of links about Saint Patrick's Day:
http://www.childsworld.com/links
NOTE TO PARENTS, TEACHERS, AND LIBRARIANS:
We routinely verify our Web links to make sure they're safe,
active sites—so encourage your readers to check them out!

ABOUT THE AUTHOR

Ann Heinrichs lives in Chicago, Illinois. She has written more than two hundred books for children. She loves traveling to faraway places.

ABOUT THE ILLUSTRATOR

Joel Snyder is a graduate of the Rhode Island School of Design. He lives in New York with his seventeen-year-old son, a beagle, and twelve tropical fish.

Index